The Shimmering World

First Sentient Publications edition 2008
Copyright © 2008 by Steven Harrison and Richard Stodart

Cover design by Kim Johansen, Black Dog Design
Cover art by Richard Stodart
Book design by Connie Shaw

Library of Congress Cataloging-in-Publication Data
Harrison, Steven, 1954–
  The shimmering world : living meditation / by Steven Harrison. -- 1st Sentient Publications
ed.
    p. cm.
 ISBN 978-1-59181-066-7
 1. Life. I. Title.

BD431.H3145 2007
128--dc22

                                    2007035246

Printed in China
10 9 8 7 6 5 4 3 2 1

SENTIENT PUBLICATIONS

A Limited Liability Company
1113 Spruce Street
Boulder, CO 80302
www.sentientpublications.com

The Shimmering World
Living Meditation

Steven Harrison

art by Richard Stodart
edited by Connie Shaw

SENTIENT PUBLICATIONS

This book is compiled from published and unpublished works of the contemporary mystic Steven Harrison. It is both an introduction to his work for those not familiar with him, and a collection of some of his most moving and penetrating statements for those who are. Its brevity and focus are intended to make it particularly useful as a tool for deep discovery. Please take these words to heart, sift them through the sieve of inquiry, and find clarity and fullness in the meditation that is your life.

—Connie Shaw, editor

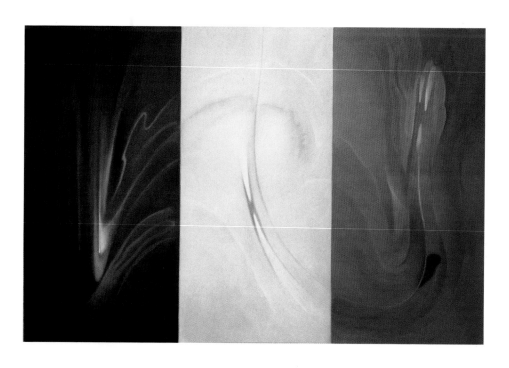

The question that life brings us is the movement of life itself, intrinsically dynamic, uncertain, and vital.

Where the question is present, there is no place for an answer to rest. Without an answer, there is no power, no authority, no answerer.

We are fascinated with the notion of understanding. We are sure the knowledge that we have accumulated through a lifetime of learning is very, very important.

It isn't.

It is very, very much in the way of direct perception. What we already know is static, but the life we seek to understand is not.

The spiritual teacher may provide us with the keys to the universe, but the universe is not locked.

The very grasping for an answer, for a response, for a solution that relieves us of the burden of feeling, is the problem. Without the grasping of the seeker, there is no solution. Without a solution, the nature of the problem fundamentally changes.

Humility is the absence of a particular position in relation to the world around us, the silencing of the critic within, the surrender to the movement of life without interpretation.

In the face of the vastness, the magic, the unknown quality of life, and in a moment of true humility, we may discover the actuality that washes away all our concepts.

In a wild moment of recognition, we look around at the world we inhabit and there is the primal experience of complete confusion. Confusion is the introduction to true intelligence – an intelligence without a center and without the dominance of thought.

We're lost in the woods. The worst thing to do is to wander around looking for the way out. Looking for a way out uses up our energy, makes us feel more and more frantic, and usually gets us even more confused and further from help.

The best thing to do when we are lost in the woods is to sit down, make a nice fire, and relax. The best thing is to wait for help to find us. If we're bored, we can make messages on the ground for airplanes to read.

We're lost in complexity. Looking for space in our life fills up the space of our life. It exhausts us and makes us feel more and more frantic and takes us further from help. Let the spaciousness of life find us.

It is always here, which is precisely where we are.

Relax. Help is very near.

We are in conflict. Stay with that fact. That conflict is vibrating; it is shaking our world. Let our world shake. Let it tumble down. Whatever is left standing is life itself. Life is not in conflict.

If we are prepared to look deeply at our conflict and not look away, we will discover that we are in a crisis of the spirit. Our life is on fire. Our life is falling away. Everything we have built and held dear is shattered. We have entered the dark night of the soul. We are prepared to die. And we are, for the first time in our lives, glimpsing freedom.

The spiritual crisis, when it visits our lives, is the moment of profound change. It is the moment when we may come to the root of our pain, the source of our existential dilemma. We do not need to fix it, we do not need to run from it, we do not need to fear it. We do not need to do anything. In doing nothing we are left with an acute awareness of all that is occurring. An acute awareness of all that is occurring is, after all, what we are.

Awareness is not the result of anything. There is nothing that causes it. There is nothing we can do to create it.

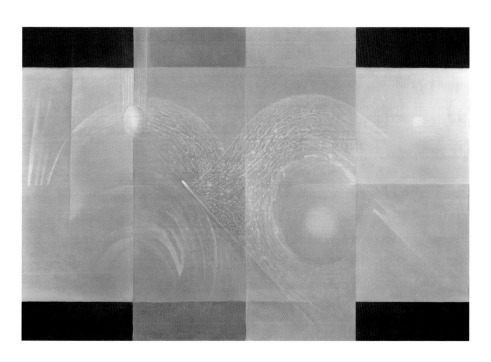

There is only one crisis, and it is a total crisis. The crisis is thought itself, our belief in it, our identification with it and with its bastard child, the "me."

We can do absolutely nothing about this "me." Doing nothing is not a technique. It can neither be taught nor learned. It cannot be practiced. The paradoxical hopelessness of the "me" realizing its own nature leaves us without an option, without a response, without a method. This stillness, without the possibility of action, without the hope for redemption, is the spontaneous realization of the truth of life.

By doing nothing we do not avoid what is happening. It is being described in the negative because it is not an action.
It is declining the action that avoids.

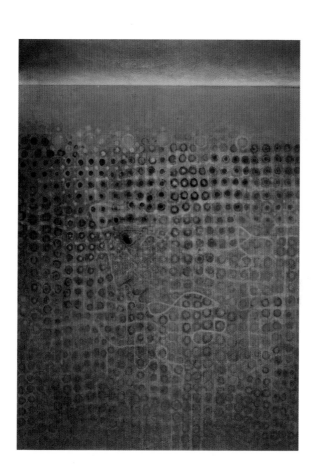

We feel conflict. We cannot turn to psychology to explain it. We cannot fix it. We cannot make it go away. The conflict we feel is not a problem. It is a messenger.

The conflict is existential. It is the friction between the bundle of ideas we call our self and the actuality of the boundarylessness of the world. We cannot learn to integrate; we can only discover that we are integrated. The conflict is the guide. If it is covered over, we lose our way to this discovery.

We do not need help; we need only understand that there is no choice in life but to follow the conflict where it takes us. If we are prepared to go there, we may discover the actuality of self and the nature of our sorrow.

The recognition of pain is the moment of freedom. Following this thread of conflict, we may come to the end of our difficulty by coming to the end of our selves.

It's not just that we don't have to change ourselves — it's that we *cannot* change ourselves. That realization is our freedom.

We may say that the world is illusion, but it is the viewer that is the illusion. The illusion is that the viewer is constant and solid.

The very nature of our existence is tenuous, hanging moment by moment, breath by breath on some invisible, evanescent quality called Life.

Death comes not just at the end of our life; it comes every moment. Look closely at the thought-body, at the mind as it creates reality through the arising of thought. Thought arises, but then it passes away. The universe is created and destroyed. Observe this carefully.

In the moment we die, in each moment we die, what is new is waiting to express.

Let the actual movement of life sweep through your life totally and you die, because there's nothing about the way you think of yourself that will survive that.

Is there a point of death, if there is no point of birth? If we cannot find a solid self in our minds or our bodies, then what is it that will dissolve in death? Is what we fear in death, the end of our separation, already a fact? What is not born cannot die. Death has already claimed that which is not actual.

Find the point of birth and at that moment death will be revealed. The alpha and omega are the same. That point of birth and death is this very moment, this very word, which falls away into absolute stillness. We know nothing about ourselves outside of the conditioned patterns. We don't know what our capacities are, or what our potential is. We don't know anything about ourselves other than that we are still, we are complete, and we are in relationship without need. We are no longer functioning in the context of life, but rather we are the expression of that context. The beauty of it is beyond description. It is beyond imagination.

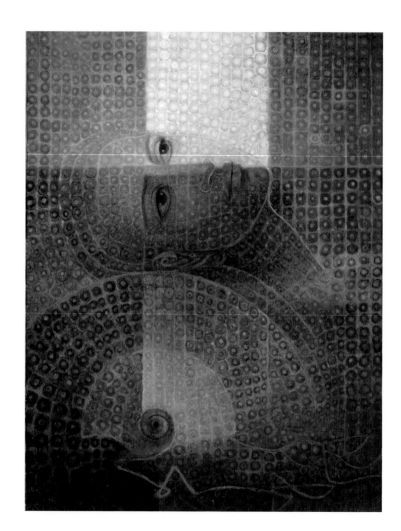

Change is the movement of energy without hindrance. It is the echo of life itself.

Change moves through us, through our habits, our resistance, our denial. Change is the truth of life.

Change is freedom. It is the end of attachment. It is the end of fear. There is nothing that binds us, there never has been.

The unknown is the portal to freedom. The life of freedom is fresh and vital simply because it is *not* the past, the repetition, the known.

Why does the unknown create such angst? The unknown is not really what it seems. It is not even unknown. What is truly unknown can generate no quality in our minds, because it does not yet have any quality. What is truly unknown cannot generate fear. What, then, is creating all of the fear by which we guide our lives?

Into the null set, the unknown, our minds project what fear tells us is there. This dark closet of our mind contains the memory of our failures, our hurts, our anxieties. This is the known, the repeating litany of the past by which we try to navigate the future. We cannot bear the thought of the unknown, not because it is empty, but because it is filled with our known. It is filled with us, and we are in pain.

Fear has looked hard at the life of freedom, feeling, and passion and declared it unfit for human habitation.

The fact is that fear is what is unfit for human habitation. Fear needs to be condemned and torn down. Yet we allow fear to operate our lives, and we live, with resignation, in the soul squalor of fear.

Love waits for fear to fall silent. Fear knows nothing about love and cannot know that love is waiting. Love is the greatest gift Fear will ever receive.

We think that if we can remove ourselves from stress, challenge, and difficulty, we will be happy. If we can rid ourselves of the screaming kid, the wife who doesn't look like she really loves us anymore, the mean boss, or the failing business, we will be happy. But we can't get rid of stress – life is inherently stressful. When we see that life is both stressful and dynamic, it's where we actually want to be *and* it's painful, then we can be happy. This is the full expression of life in this moment. There's no other place to go or be – the full texture of life is happening in the explosion out of this one moment.

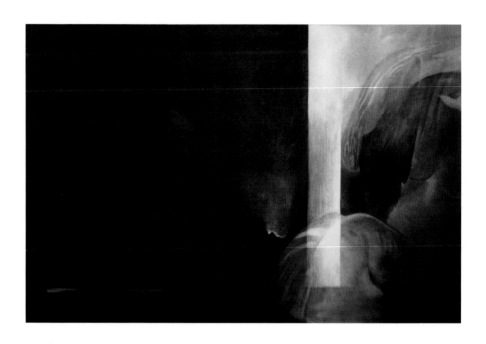

We are on the cutting edge, the brink, the edge of the abyss each and every moment. There are no guarantees to give and none to get. We are fully responsible for the entirety of our life.

Happiness grows only out of the profound silence in which the thoughts we call our self arise. In the moment our thoughts come still and just before the next thought arises — there, just there, is happiness. There, in the vast quiet, just there, is relationship.

Like archaeologists of the soul, we begin to uncover the debris of our mind. Our need to exist in full relationship to our world is what drives us. The layer upon layer of ideas, conditioning, and fear is what we dig through. In this search we have somehow forgotten that we have forgotten. The search has taken on a life of its own. The search has given us meaning that substitutes for what we have forgotten. But searching for love will not replace love. Nothing will replace love. If we forget everything else, let us remember that.

We know that we are both the teller of the tale and the expression of the story itself. We know that we are the meeting point of heaven and earth, the divine and the comic, the relative and the absolute. We can experience the divine in the depths of our humanness. We have the capacity to love.

ᜒ

The hubris of knowledge must be the first sacrifice. For it, we get nothing in return. Nothing is a great gift indeed.

The world does not disappear in emptiness. It occurs in emptiness, and it is transformed by the recognition of emptiness.

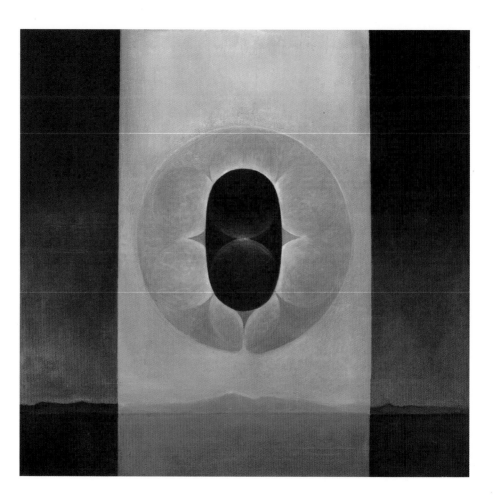

If we pay attention to the field of consciousness in which thought arises, we can find no separation. The field of consciousness is apparently boundaryless. This vast, undivided awareness is available to us at all times. It is there at any moment we are still. It is as present in us as our thoughts. But we identify with thoughts, which are limited and separating by nature. Why is it that we do not identify with the field of consciousness, the milieu in which these thoughts arise?

We can't find a self, a center, a "me," no matter how hard we try. We seem to be made up of, well, nothing.

Buddha was not just suggesting that we are nothing, he was pointing out that because we are nothing, we are everything. That's a lot.

We are terrified by the understanding that we are actually the universe. We are the power, the glory, the wisdom, the everything.

Jesus put the icing on the cake by directing us to love our neighbor as ourselves, which is about all we have left to do when we are nothing.

We are the human condition. And, knowing this, unavoidably we find compassion, connection, we fall in love.

We fall in love with ourselves, with each other, with the human condition.

Love, in the end, doesn't come from being loving. It comes from being human. It comes from our failure to love and from our fear of love. The mythic Jesus, after all, was incarnate as a human being. He had all the passions of a human and all the failures. In between some fairly impressive miracles, he perceived that the other is ourself. That's the miracle.

Love is the fire that burns us. We cannot survive; we cannot be there when something new emerges from the ashes, takes wing, and flies. This is why although we say we want love, in fact, we fear love.

The expression of love, all-encompassing, non-separate love, cannot be absorbed. It shatters the other as it shatters us. It is the most powerful and the most avoided energy. In love there is no "me." The parasite dies; the host lives.

Love is everything and, as such, cannot be contained by anything.

Love is a description of what is beyond words.

In love we are in relationship and, in relationship, everything is in contact with everything else, everything is part of everything else. We are not separate in love, and in truth, what we love is our separation. We cannot give it up, even though it is destroying us.

Aloneness is fearless. It is the ground on which we may enter into relationship with the world around us.
Aloneness has the integrity of needing nothing.

Aloneness is the transformer through which consciousness flows to become love. This love is the message of the universe. It is the truth of the universe. Yet, it cannot be touched by those who crave, who desire, who want. Only when we have found the absolute contentment of aloneness can we give expression to love. This is our purification.

All those who are inquiring stand alone in the universe. There is no reliable support, there is only our integrity as a guide. Even relationships forged in the understanding of this exploration, by their nature, must challenge, not coddle us.

Deep questioning of our existence is not for the fainthearted or the dilettante. Such exploration will disrupt, transform, and change the entirety of our perspective, because the perspective comes from a "me" that isn't there. This thin veil of illusion, once pierced, will always be pierced.

No one can give us directions on how to live with integrity. No one can certify that we are living our perceptions.

No authority can answer our question, but perhaps we will be fortunate and discover someone who will question our answer.

We stand alone, where we are. This is the portal to the whole of life.

The whole does not require us to figure it out, only that we live in the fullness of life. Our inquiry is not just the search for an explanation but the discovery of life itself in the actuality of each moment.

There is nothing outside of everything. All that we are left with is being. Being has no subject or object. It has no "thingness." Being subsumes everything. It is the universe as it is.

In being, there is only unity. It is the Self that the self forgot in early childhood. It is the love that we all seek in relationship to another. It is the mystic expression that religion seeks to convey.

In being, we discover our Self in relationship — not a relationship of time and space, but of two melded into one, self into Self, doing into being.

When we breathe, the universe breathes.

We saw in the beloved such promise, such beauty. We had such a direct experience of love, of expansion, of openness when we met.

We have only looked for this expanded feeling in another. We have never looked within our life as it is. We have never asked ourselves whether this vast feeling of connectedness, of safety, of surety, is available now, here, without anything, without another.

If this expanded feeling, this sense of love is not causative, if it does not occur because of something, then we are freed from the burden of acting, of doing, or searching. We do not need to find someone to give us love. We have love already. We are immersed in it. We cannot avoid it. The only way we can miss the fact of love is by searching for it, by looking for someone who can give it to us.

We are conditioned to this notion of another who will give us love. We believe with all our being that we have found love when we find the other. We have not found love. We have found a hopelessly flawed projection. We have found an impossible image. We have found an other who cannot possibly give us what we already have, what we have always had, and what we will always have. We have found the obscuration of our vision, the forgetting of our love, the overwhelming sleepiness of conditioning.

We have not found love. We have found contraction. We have shrunk the expansiveness of the universe into a bubble world consisting of me and the other. We become the center of the bubble, and all we see is a reflection of that center on the inner surface of the bubble. The shimmering world is perfect, it is just as we had hoped, it is all and everything. Then the bubble bursts.

One of the curses of human existence is the tendency to misconstrue language for actuality. Relationship has nothing to do with language, name, or concept. We cannot control relationship. We are already in relationship, but our view is so obscured that we do not recognize that fact.

If we are particularly alert, sensitive, and open, we may discover this fact. We are already in relationship.

If we have not discovered this, if we do not fundamentally experience this in our moment-to-moment existence, then we have fallen victim to the great curse. We are stuck in language, concept, thought. We are entombed in our own brains.

We are *thinking* our lives, not *living* them. We are thinking love and relationship, not living them.

The construction of thought in the face of the immensity of life is an absurd attempt to come up with a strategy. We think this rather pathetic attempt at construction is a plan that gives us safety and surety. Instead, it's the denial of the absolute power of life.

Thought has nowhere to go but its own isolated, endless, fragmented repetition.

Where are we going? We have nothing, which is what we have always had. There is no vantage point, but there is space. This space is not a concept (although we can try hard to make it one). It is empty of concept, empty of us.

This space transcends us, because it transcends our concepts. This space connects us, because in this space all actuality exists related not in a conceptual framework but in existential reality.

We have lost ourselves in nothing, and we have found our existence stripped bare of everything but its interrelatedness. We are not *in* relationship, we *are* relationship. In this moment we glimpse that this is the simple nature of what is. It has always been so, with or without our view or understanding.

This radically changes relationship to another, because we find no entry point to relationship and no exit from it. We cannot look for relationship; there is nothing to see that is not already in relationship. We cannot get anything from relationship; we already hold everything. We have no place to go and nothing to do.

When we come to love, we must throw out this last thing, this last idea. Whatever we call love, we must throw it out. Throw out the good feeling around the word; throw out the bad feeling for not having the word.

Throw out love. It is not actual. There is nothing that is love. Nothing is love. Love is nothing.

This is the frontier beyond which nothing can help us — no teacher, no theory, no philosophy, no book.
This is the space beyond language and beyond us.

It cannot be described. It can only be lived. Life exists in wholeness arising spontaneously, without words, without thought, without love.

We have entered the realm of radical creativity where our art becomes the life we live, the forms we express, the very communication of the undivided energy we have discovered through the living experiment of our self.

We don't know anything about the creative space and that is the beauty, passion, and energy of it. That is why it's so alive.

Unless we reside within a belief system, we cannot find the criteria for failure. A life without authority puts us in direct contact with the effect of our life, our actions, our thoughts and feelings. Without the screen of belief we have direct perception of the world in which we exist.

How do we live without belief? We live without the conflict of my ideas with your ideas. We live without the competition of self with other. We live without resistance to the movement of life.

In the moment that we relinquish all authority, all conditioning, all projections of memory, both inner and outer, we are an empty vessel that is filled spontaneously with life itself.

✼

Walls that divide us from life take effort. Maintaining barriers requires energy. Openness is simple relaxation, letting go and giving up. The message of life will come through clearly in this state of openness.

The meditation of where we are is not even spiritual. It is life itself, moving of its own accord, fluid, quiet, beautiful, and self-fulfilled.

We live in the dynamic potential of existence, exploding in each moment, unpredictable, uncontrollable, and incredibly beautiful, and then fading into the profound silence of the universe. Faith is the recognition of the life force that animates this endless cycle of creation and decay.

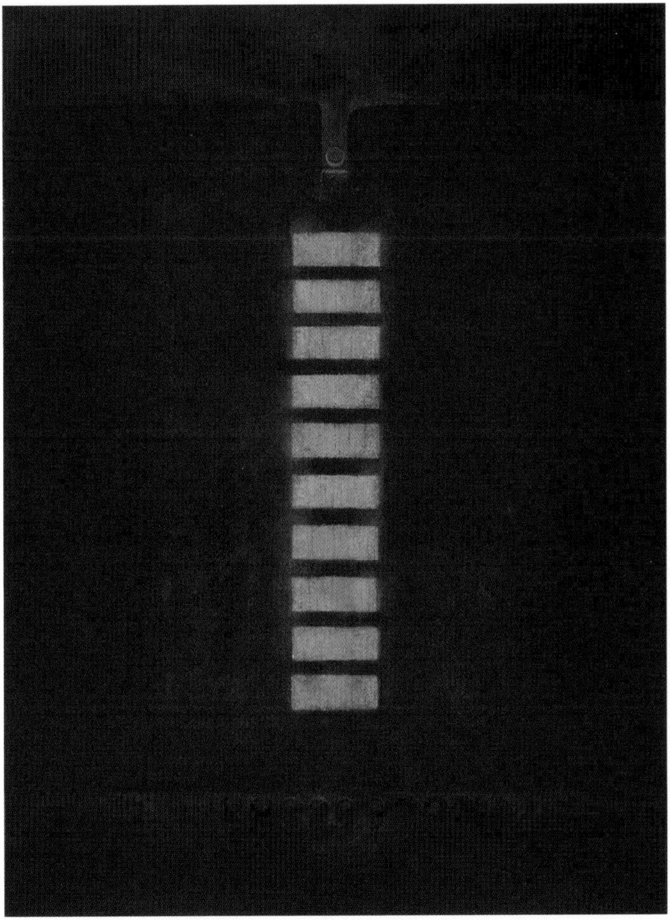

ABOUT THE AUTHOR

Steven Harrison is the author of *Doing Nothing, Being One, Getting to Where You Are, The Question to Life's Answers, The Happy Child,* and *What's Next After Now?*

ABOUT THE ARTIST

A native of Trinidad, the West Indies, Richard Stodart is a Canadian citizen and a graduate of Ryerson University in Toronto. He began painting in 1973 and in 1975 was awarded a Canada Council Grant for his paintings. Since 1976 he has lived in the United States.

The aim of Richard's work is to explore and present the freedom of dual and nondual unity. Many sources inspire him, including the spiritual teachings of Hinduism, Buddhism, Taoism, and Kabbalism.

Richard's art has appeared on magazine, book, and music album covers. His paintings have been exhibited in galleries in Canada, Hawaii, and the US mainland. He is the author of *Free and Easy Wandering, Markings on the Way*. Visit his website: www.richardstodart.com.

PAINTING TITLES

Cover	Being and Acting as the Creative Center of the Universe
Title page	Moon Over Trinidad
"The question that life brings..."	Trikaya
"When the question is present..."	Full Moon and Clouds
"In a wild moment..."	Sky Dancer
"We're lost in the woods..."	I Ching
"Awareness is..."	Demonstration of Great Order
"By doing nothing..."	Light Riddle
"It's not just that we ..."	Emergence
"We may say..."	Light Matrix
"The very nature of..."	Sower's Seeds
"Change is the movement..."	She Wakens
"We are on the cutting edge..."	Prometheus
"The world does not disappear..."	Black Sun
"If we pay attention..."	Immortality
"We can't find a self..."	Chrystal Buddha
"Jesus put the..."	Transfiguration of Christ

"Love is the fire..."   Of an Ancient Civilization

"Aloneness is fearless..."   The Muse

"Aloneness is the transformer..."   Goddess of Purification

"When we breathe..."   Immortal Air

"We have not found love..."   Tiny Geometries

"When we come to love..."   Red Couple

"We have entered the realm..."   Immortal Water

"We live in the dynamic..."   Stupa

Sentient Publications, LLC publishes books on cultural creativity, experimental education, transformative spirituality, holistic health, new science, ecology, and other topics, approached from an integral viewpoint. Our authors are intensely interested in exploring the nature of life from fresh perspectives, addressing life's great questions, and fostering the full expression of the human potential. Sentient Publications' books arise from the spirit of inquiry and the richness of the inherent dialogue between writer and reader.

Our Culture Tools series is designed to give social catalyzers and cultural entrepreneurs the essential information, technology, and inspiration to forge a sustainable, creative, and compassionate world.

We are very interested in hearing from our readers. To direct suggestions or comments to us, or to be added to our mailing list, please contact:

SENTIENT PUBLICATIONS, LLC
1113 Spruce Street
Boulder, CO 80302
303-443-2188
contact@sentientpublications.com
www.sentientpublications.com

Book

Cynthia Cousins & Karen King

Illustrated by **Susan David**

Prepared from the archives and resources
of Shady Maple Farms.

First published in Canada in 1997 by
Raincoast Books
8680 Cambie Street
Vancouver, B.C.
V6P 6M9
(604) 323-7100
First published in 1997 by The Appletree Press Ltd.
Copyright © 1997 The Appletree Press Ltd.
and Shady Maple Farms.
Printed in the U.A.E. All rights reserved.
No part of this publication may be reproduced or
transmitted in any form or by any means, electronic or
mechanical, photocopying, recording or any information
and retrieval system, without permission
in writing from the publisher.

Canadian Cataloguing in Publication Data

Cousins, Cynthia.
A little Canadian maple syrup book

ISBN 1-55192-062-X

1. Cookery (Maple sugar and syrup)
2. Maple syrup. I. King, Karen, 1943- II. Title.
TX767.M3C68 1997   641.6'364   C96-910764-1

9 8 7 6 5 4 3 2 1

A Note on Measures
Spoon measurements are level unless otherwise indicated.

Maple Syrup - Magnifique!

Natural sap dripping from sugar maple trees is one sure sign for many eastern Canadians that spring has arrived. For those who grew up with sugaring off parties, the taste of maple syrup boiled down into a thick taffy served on fresh white snow will always be a wonderful memory.

Maple Syrup: In the Beginning

It was aboriginal Canadians who first discovered the secret of tapping maple trees to gather maple sugar. An early aboriginal legend tells how the god Nanabozho believed the taste of maple syrup was so extraordinary that its value would be underrated by humans if it was too accessible. So he added water to the viscous syrup to make it watery and hid it deep inside glorious trees. Since then, getting syrup from the maple tree has been no easy task.

In the beginning, aboriginals collected sap from maple trees by making a diagonal cut in the trunk and inserting a bark spout in the gash. The sap flowed through the spout and was caught in birch bark buckets.

The primitive evaporation process began when the sap was poured into hollowed-out basswood logs to which hot rocks were added. Slowly the sap became a syrup, then toffee and then a crude dark sugar.

Maple sugar was the cheapest and generally the only accessible sweetener in Canada until the mid 1800's. The aboriginals taught early pioneers how to gather the sweet maple nectar and heat it until it was concentrated into a golden amber syrup.

The simple art of gathering maple syrup was passed down through generations to become part of Canada's heritage. Today the process has become more sophisticated but maple syrup remains a 100% pure organic product derived directly from nature.

Maple Syrup: The Secret Within the Maple Tree

Maple syrup is made from a special seasonal secretion. This sweet water sap is different from the circulatory sap of the growing tree. The special maple sap flows in spring when the weather shifts from freezing to thawing temperatures. If the weather remains either too warm or too cold, the maple sap will slow down or come to a standstill. For this reason, weather watching is a necessity for maple sap collection. When the climate is favourable, sap may flow for as long as six weeks. Poor weather conditions may result in a short run for as little as five days. Syrup season may begin as early as March or as late as mid-April, so maple farmers must be prepared to tap the tree when nature is ready.

There are several varieties of maple trees in North America, eastern Asia and China, but it is the sugar maple that is the most productive and gives the best syrup. These trees can live to be 250 years old, but they are usually 30 years old and 10 inches (25 cm) in diameter before they can be tapped. Since tapping does no permanent damage to the tree, it may well be that some

trees that were tapped by early settlers are still giving sap today. Although the life span of the sugar maple is long, the yield is not plentiful. Each tap yields only about 1.76 pints (one litre) of syrup per season.

Up until 25 years ago, the majority of maple producers used pails to collect their sap. Today most producers have moved to a collection method of tubes under vacuum. These systems increase the yield without affecting the tree growth and allow tapping earlier in the season.

While today's maple syrup harvesting employs modern technology and high-capacity evaporators, pure maple syrup remains an all-natural unrefined sweetener.

Maple Syrup's Nutritional Content

When first tapped, maple sap is about 97% water, 3% maple sugar and 0.1% minerals. The bottled pure maple syrup is 34% water, 66% maple sugar with 40 calories per tablespoon (15 ml). Minerals in pure maple syrup include calcium, potassium, magnesium, manganese, phosphorus and iron. Trace amount of vitamins, including riboflavin, pantothenic acid, pyridoxine, niacin and folic acid, are also present .

Breakfast and Brunch

Turn a routine breakfast into a special treat, by adding pure maple syrup. Warm up maple syrup and drizzle it over pancakes, waffles, cereal, French toast or grapefruit. Try sweetening tea or coffee by adding a teaspoon (5 ml) of maple syrup. Or add pure maple syrup to sour cream or yoghurt for a delicious topping for strawberries, blueberries or raspberries.

Easy Baked Cinnamon Toast

This baked French toast puffs up in the oven to resemble a soufflé. Garnish with orange slices and strawberries for a festive, but easy, brunch.

2 tsp/10 g butter
8 slices crusty bread, at least 1 inch /2.5 cm thick
8 eggs
1 1/4 pts/750 ml milk
6 fl oz/175 ml pure maple syrup
1/2 tsp/2 ml cinnamon
1/2 tsp/2 ml nutmeg
icing sugar (optional)
(serves 4)

Preheat oven to 350°F (180°C). Butter a 9 x 13 inch (22 x 32 cm) baking dish. Place the bread snugly into the baking dish, adding more bread if required. Lightly beat the eggs, then stir in the milk, maple syrup, cinnamon and nutmeg. Pour the mixture over the bread. Bake uncovered for about 55–60 minutes, or until golden brown and the centre is set. Sprinkle with icing sugar or drizzle with additional maple syrup. Serve immediately.

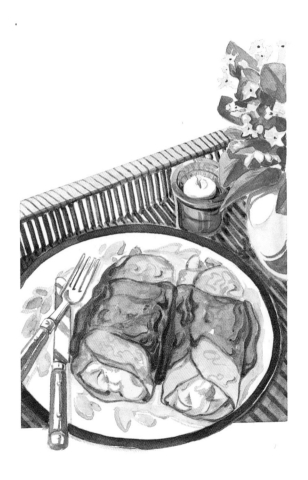

Crêpes with Ricotta and Peach Filling

The peaches and ricotta cheese team together well in these delicious crêpes.

Crêpes	Filling
5 oz/150 g plain flour	5 large peaches
12 fl oz/375 ml milk	2 tbsp/30 g butter
1 tbsp/15 ml pure maple syrup	8 fl oz/250 ml pure maple syrup
3 eggs	8 oz/240 g ricotta cheese
2 tbsp/30 ml vegetable oil	2 tsp/10 ml grated lemon rind
vegetable oil for frying	
(serves 4–6)	

Crêpes: In a large bowl, whisk together the flour, milk, maple syrup, eggs and oil. Allow to stand for 10–15 minutes. Heat an 8 inch (20 cm) crêpe pan or non-stick frying pan, then brush with a little oil. Pour about 4 fl oz (125 ml) of the batter into the pan, tilting to spread the batter. Cook for 1 minute until lightly brown, then turn and cook the remaining side until it is also lightly brown. Repeat until all batter is used. Stack crêpes, cover loosely and keep warm.

Filling: Peel the peaches and slice thinly. Heat the butter and syrup in a non-stick frying pan over a medium heat. Add the peaches. Cook, uncovered, until the peaches are tender, approximately 5 minutes. Remove the peaches and keep them warm. Pour the syrup into a heatproof jug. Stir together the ricotta cheese, lemon rind and 1 fl oz (30 ml) of the syrup. Fill each crêpe with about 1 tbsp (15 g) of the cheese mixture and about 4 peach slices. Roll up and top with the remaining peach slices. Pour the remaining syrup over the crêpes and serve.

Maple Cinnamon Buns

The aroma of these cinnamon buns will evoke images of cozy family kitchens.

4 fl oz/125 ml milk	1 tbsp/15 g dry yeast
1 1/2 fl oz/50 ml pure maple syrup	2 eggs, beaten
4.5 oz/135 g butter	1 1/4 lb/600 g plain flour
1 tsp/5 ml salt	1 tsp/5 ml cinnamon
1 tsp/5 ml sugar	2 oz/60 g raisins and/or pecans
4 fl oz/125 ml warm water	3 tbsp/45 g brown sugar
(makes 9 buns)	

In a small saucepan, heat the milk, maple syrup, 2 1/2 oz (75 g) butter and salt until lukewarm. Meanwhile, dissolve the sugar in warm water; sprinkle in the yeast and allow to stand for 10 minutes. In a large bowl, combine the milk and yeast mixtures with the eggs. Beat in 15 oz (450 g) of flour until smooth. Gradually add the remaining flour to make a soft, sticky dough. Knead on a lightly floured surface for 5 minutes or until smooth and elastic. Shape into a smooth ball and place in a large greased bowl. Cover and set aside until doubled in size, about 1 1/2 hours. Punch down. Roll dough into an 8 x 10 inch (20 x 25 cm) rectangle. Spread with 2 tbsp (30 g) of softened butter and sprinkle with cinnamon. Cover with raisins and/or pecans. Roll up from long side and cut into 9 slices. Combine 2 tbsp (30 g) of melted butter with 3 tbsp (45 g) of brown sugar in a 9 inch (25 cm) square cake pan and place the dough slices, cut side down, on top. Cover and allow to rise until doubled, approximately 45 minutes. Bake at 375°F (190°C) for 25 minutes or until golden brown. Turn immediately onto serving plate.

Apricot Date Loaf

A tasty loaf for brunch with the hint of maple accented by the flavour of apricots and dates.

---

5 oz/150 g plain flour
3 oz/90 g whole-wheat flour
1 tsp/5 ml baking powder
$^1/_2$ tsp/2 ml baking soda
1 tsp/5 ml salt
2 tsp/10 ml cinnamon
6 fl oz/175 ml pure maple syrup
6 fl oz/175 ml buttermilk
$1^1/_2$ fl oz/50 ml vegetable oil
2 eggs, lightly beaten
1 tsp/5 ml vanilla
$2^1/_2$ oz/75 g dried apricots, chopped
$2^1/_2$ oz/75 g dates, chopped
(makes 1 loaf)

In a small mixing bowl, mix the flour, baking powder, baking soda, salt and cinnamon together. In a large mixing bowl, stir together the maple syrup, buttermilk, vegetable oil, eggs and vanilla. Add the flour mixture and stir until combined. Add the apricots and dates. Pour into a well greased 9 x 5 inch (23 x 13 cm) loaf pan. Bake at 350°F (180°C) for 50 minutes or until a skewer inserted in the centre comes out clean. Cool in the loaf pan for 10 minutes, then turn onto a cooling rack.

Vegetables and Salads

Enhance the flavour of "ordinary vegetables" with pure maple syrup. The hearty flavour of cabbage, string beans and parsnips will benefit most from this unique sweet nutty taste. Combine two tablespoons (30 ml) each of maple syrup and butter together and use as a glaze to enhance the humblest vegetable.

In salad dressings, use maple syrup as the sweetener. Vary the dressing ingredients to create new salad sensations every day.

Maple Classic Dressing

A hint of maple flavour adds complexity to a simple dressing.

2¹/₂ fl oz/75 ml cider or balsamic vinegar
3 tbsp/45 ml pure maple syrup
1 tbsp/15 ml Dijon mustard
1 clove garlic, crushed
pinch of freshly ground black pepper
4 fl oz/125 ml olive oil
(makes 8 fl oz / 250 ml)

Whisk together the vinegar, maple syrup, mustard, garlic and pepper. Gradually whisk in the oil. Drizzle the dressing over salad greens and toss before serving. Refrigerate the remaining dressing.

Maple Spiced Dressing

Horseradish adds a zesty flavour to this elegant maple dressing.

2¹/₂ fl oz/75 ml red wine vinegar
3 tbsp/45 ml pure maple syrup
2 tbsp/30 ml horseradish
4 fl oz/125 ml vegetable oil
(makes 8 fl oz / 250 ml)

Whisk together the vinegar, maple syrup and horseradish. Gradually whisk in the oil. Drizzle the dressing over salad greens and toss before serving. Refrigerate the remaining dressing.

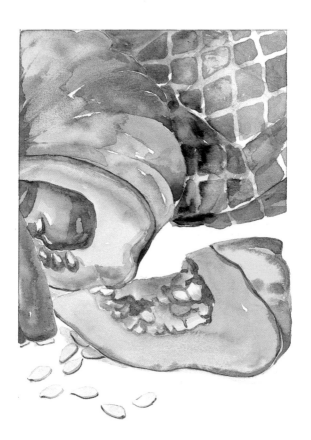

Citrus Baked Squash

For variation, you can omit the orange rind in this recipe and sprinkle each piece of squash with freshly ground nutmeg instead.

---

³/₄ lb/875 g acorn or pepper squash
2 tsp/10 ml butter
1¹/₂ fl oz/50 ml pure maple syrup
1 tsp/5 ml orange rind, finely grated
4 fl oz/125 ml water
(serves 4)

Cut the squash in half lengthways and scoop out the seeds. Cut in half again to have four serving pieces. Place the squash pieces in a baking dish. Put ¹/₂ tsp (2 ml) butter, 1 tbsp (15 ml) maple syrup and ¹/₄ tsp (1 ml) orange rind into each cavity. Pour the water into the baking dish. Bake at 350°F (180°C) for 45 minutes, or until tender.

Glazed Carrots

Ginger adds heat to this simple dish, while thyme adds flavour and visual appeal.

---

1 lb/500 g carrots, cleaned and sliced thickly on diagonal
1 tbsp/15 ml butter
3 tbsp/45 ml pure maple syrup
¹/₄ tsp/1 ml ground ginger
¹/₄ tsp/1 ml thyme leaves
(serves 4)

Cook the carrots in salted boiling water for about 10 minutes until tender-crisp. Drain thoroughly. Add the butter, maple syrup, ginger and thyme to the carrots. Cook, uncovered, on a medium heat until the syrup boils. Continue cooking uncovered until the syrup is reduced and thickened and the carrots are glazed, approximately 5 minutes.

Broccoli in Maple Walnut Vinaigrette

Walnut oil adds a very distinctive flavour, but it can be replaced by corn oil if necessary.

---

1 large bunch broccoli
2 tbsp/30 ml red wine vinegar
2 tbsp/30 ml pure maple syrup
1 tsp/5 ml Dijon mustard
2 tbsp/30 ml walnut oil
1 1/2 oz/45 g chopped walnuts
(serves 4–5)

Wash the broccoli and cut into florets. Cook until tender-crisp in boiling, salted water. Meanwhile, whisk together the vinegar, maple syrup and mustard. Gradually whisk in the walnut oil. Place the cooked broccoli in a shallow serving dish. Pour the vinaigrette over the broccoli and sprinkle with walnuts. Serve immediately.

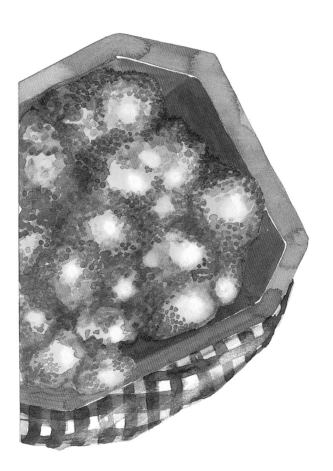

Four Bean Salad

Maple syrup acts as a unique sweetener in this colourful and nutritious salad.

---

¹/₄ pt/150 ml tarragon or white wine vinegar
4 fl oz/125 ml vegetable oil
2¹/₂ fl oz/75 ml pure maple syrup
1 tsp/5 ml dry mustard
³/₄ tsp/3 ml dried tarragon
¹/₂ tsp/2 ml freshly ground pepper
1 tin (19 fl oz/540 ml) red kidney beans
1 tin (19 fl oz/540 ml) white kidney beans
1 tin (19 fl oz/540 ml) chick peas
1 tin (14 fl oz/398 ml) cut green beans
5 oz/150 g celery, sliced
1 medium sweet red pepper, chopped
2 green onions, sliced
(serves 10–12)

In a small bowl, whisk together the vinegar, oil, maple syrup, mustard, tarragon and pepper. Drain the tins of red kidney beans, white kidney beans, chick peas and green beans. Rinse the beans with cold water, then mix in a large bowl. Add the celery, red pepper and green onions. Pour the oil and vinegar mixture over the beans and mix well. Cover and refrigerate for at least 8 hours or overnight, stirring occasionally. Drain before serving.

Meat, Poultry and Legumes

Nothing beats maple syrup for glazing ham, ribs and poultry. Whether it is teamed with the piquant taste of dry mustard, orange rind or ginger, the unique flavour of maple syrup always complements a roasted, grilled or barbecued meat dish.

As a meat marinade, maple syrup adds flavour and texture. Vary the marinade ingredients to create subtle or distinctive flavours.

Lemon Rosemary Marinated Chicken

This marinade is perfect for boneless chicken breasts. Try to use fresh rosemary as it gives the best flavour. Lime juice may be substituted for lemon juice.

2½ fl oz/75 ml lemon juice	1 clove garlic, minced
3 tbsp/45 ml vegetable oil	4 boneless chicken breasts
2 tbsp/30 ml fresh rosemary	2 fl oz/60 ml pure maple syrup
(or 1 tsp/5 ml dried)	2 tbsp/30 ml Dijon mustard

Whisk together the lemon juice, vegetable oil, rosemary and garlic. Pour the marinade over the chicken and marinate for at least 2 hours in a refrigerator. Drain the chicken, reserving marinade. Blend the maple syrup and Dijon mustard into the reserved marinade and baste the chicken frequently during grilling or barbecuing.

Peanut Grilling Sauce

Peanut sauce adds a popular Asian taste to any barbecue. Especially good with pork chops or chicken breasts.

2 oz/60 g peanut butter
2 fl oz/60 ml lemon juice or white vinegar
2 fl oz/60 ml pure maple syrup
2 cloves garlic, minced
1 tbsp/15 ml sesame oil

Whisk together all ingredients. Marinate meat or poultry in the sauce for at least 2 hours in a refrigerator. Drain and use the reserved marinade as a basting sauce during the last 10 minutes of grilling or barbecuing.

Crispy Maple Ribs

Maple syrup enhances the flavour of these succulent ribs.

3 lb/1.5 kg pork spare ribs
6 fl oz/175 ml pure maple syrup
1 tbsp/15 ml ketchup
1 tbsp/15 ml Worcestershire sauce
1 tbsp/15 ml red wine vinegar
1 clove garlic, finely minced
1/2 tsp/2 ml dry mustard
pinch of salt
(serves 4–6)

Cut ribs into serving-size pieces, then place in a large saucepan and cover with water. Boil gently, covered, for about 1 hour or until tender, then drain. In a small saucepan, stir together the remaining ingredients. Bring to a boil. Pour over the ribs. Marinate in a refrigerator for about 2 hours, then remove the ribs and reserve marinade. Bake at 350°F (180°C) for 30–40 minutes, basting occasionally. Alternatively grill or barbecue for about 15 minutes until tender and glazed. Turn often and baste frequently with the sauce.

Zesty Chicken Wings

Perfect for casual get-togethers; drumsticks also work well in this recipe.

---

2 lb/1 kg chicken wings
4 fl oz/125 ml pure maple syrup
1 clove garlic, minced
1 small onion, finely chopped
2 tbsp/30 ml white vinegar
2¹/₂ fl oz/75 ml ketchup
1 tbsp/15 ml Dijon mustard
1 tsp/5 ml Worcestershire sauce
(serves 4)

Remove the tips from the chicken wings (reserve for making stock, if desired). Cut wings at joint into 2 pieces. In a shallow dish, combine the remaining ingredients, then pour over the chicken. Marinate the chicken wings in a refrigerator for at least 4 hours, turning occasionally. Transfer the wings to a greased, shallow baking dish. Arrange in a single layer and bake at 375°F (190°C) for 35–40 minutes, basting occasionally. Alternatively grill or barbecue the wings until thoroughly cooked.

Oriental Glazed Chicken

A perfect dish for the family or for entertaining. Serve with fluffy steamed rice and garnish with chopped green onions.

6 boneless chicken breasts	3 tbsp/45 ml white wine vinegar
3 tbsp/45 ml plain flour	2 fl oz/60 ml soy sauce
2 tbsp/30 ml vegetable oil	1 large clove garlic, minced
6 fl oz/175 ml pure maple syrup	2 tsp/10 ml ground ginger
2 fl oz/60 ml white wine	pinch of freshly ground pepper
(serves 6)	

Dredge the chicken breasts with flour, then shake off any excess. Heat the oil in a large, non-stick frying pan over a medium to high heat. Brown the chicken on each side. Meanwhile, whisk together the remaining ingredients. Pour the glaze mixture over the chicken breasts. Bring to a boil. Reduce heat and simmer, covered, for 30 minutes. Turn and baste chicken.

Orange Maple Glazed Duck

This simple, yet elegant, main dish is a long-established favourite.

4–5 lb/2–2.5 kg duck	3 tbsp/45 ml pure maple syrup
pinch of salt and pepper	1 orange, reserving juice and rind

For even cooking, ensure the duck is at room temperature before roasting. Preheat oven to 450°F (230°C). Prick the duck skin with a fork so the fat will drain out. Season, inside and out, with salt and pepper and place in a shallow roasting dish. Roast, uncovered, for 30 minutes. Meanwhile, combine the maple syrup with the grated rind and orange juice. Drain the fat from the dish and reduce the oven temperature to 350°F (180°C). Continue roasting, uncovered, for 1½ hours, basting with the maple syrup mixture every 10 minutes. To test if the duck is cooked, prick the skin; juices should run clear yellow and the drumstick should move easily.

Festive Maple Glazed Ham

A holiday favourite, this maple syrup glaze is very easy to make and adds a special touch to a family meal.

4 lb/2 kg ready-to-serve ham	4 fl oz/125 ml white wine
15 whole cloves	or apple juice
2½ fl oz/75 ml pure maple syrup	4 fl oz/125 ml water
1½ tsp/7 ml dry mustard	
(serves 6–8)	

Place the ham in a shallow roasting dish, fat side up. Score the fat in a diamond pattern and insert cloves into the scored ham. Combine the maple syrup and mustard together, brush half of this mixture over the ham. Pour the wine or apple juice and water into the bottom of the roasting dish. Bake at 325°F (160°C) for 1 hour, basting occasionally with the remaining maple syrup mixture. Add more water or wine, if necessary, to keep the pan from drying.

French Canadian Baked Beans

Old-fashioned, heartwarming French Canadian-style baked beans; a perfect "in from the cold" meal.

1 lb/500 g dried white pea beans	6 fl oz/175 ml pure maple syrup
3 pts/1.8 L cold water	4 fl oz/125 ml salsa
1 large onion, chopped	3 tbsp/45 ml molasses
4 oz/120 g salt pork or bacon	1 tsp/5 ml dry mustard
3 apples, peeled, cored, and cut in pieces	1 tsp/5 ml salt

(serves 8)

Rinse the beans and place in a large saucepan. Cover with cold water and allow to soak overnight. Then bring the beans to a boil (do not change the water). Reduce heat and simmer, covered, until tender, approximately 1 hour. Drain beans and reserve the cooking water. In a 3 pint (1.8 L) casserole or baking dish, combine the beans, onions, diced salt pork, apples, maple syrup, salsa, molasses, mustard and salt. Add just enough reserved cooking water to cover, then stir well. Cover and bake at 300°F (150°C) for 4 hours or until tender. Stir occasionally and add more water as required to keep the beans just covered. About 30 minutes before serving, remove lid to allow beans to brown.

Desserts

Why serve a dessert unless it has some magic? Let pure maple syrup create a stir of interest in the finale to your meals. Try adding a maple coulis to a simple dessert to make it special. Drizzle pure maple syrup on a plate, then swirl fresh fruit puree or yogurt on top before adding ice cream, cake or fresh fruit.

Creamy Dessert Fondue

This delectable fondue sauce dresses up a variety of fruits, yet is a casual dessert to share among friends.

---

1 tbsp/15 ml cornflour
1/2 pt/300 ml single cream
4 fl oz/125 ml pure maple syrup
1 tbsp/15 ml almond or fruit-flavoured liqueur
bite-size pieces of fruit for dipping (strawberries,
apple, banana, cantaloupe)
(serves 3–4)

Whisk together the cornflour and 2 tbsp (30 ml) of cream. In a medium saucepan combine the remaining cream and maple syrup. Bring just to a boil. Add the cornflour mixture and stir until thickened. Remove from the heat and stir in the liqueur. Serve in a small dessert fondue pot with fruit arranged on a platter.

Fresh Fruit Salad with Maple Syrup

A sophisticated and elegant twist on a very simple dessert.

---

4 fl oz/125 ml pure maple syrup
3 tbsp/45 ml orange or almond flavoured liqueur or rum or cognac
1 lb/500 g fresh fruit pieces (grapefruit, orange, banana,
strawberries, cantaloupe, blueberries, kiwi fruit, etc.)
(serves 5)

Mix maple syrup and liqueur together. Gently stir maple syrup mixture into fresh fruit pieces. Allow to stand for 30 minutes to 1 hour.

Maple Nut Baked Apples

Here is a twist on a comfortable old favourite. Dried cranberries are gaining popularity and make for a colourful and delicious alternative to raisins.

---

4 apples
4 fl oz/125 ml pure maple syrup
1 tbsp/15 ml chopped pecans or almond slivers
1 tbsp/15 ml raisins or dried cranberries
1 tbsp/15 g butter
1 tsp/5 ml cinnamon
water
(serves 4)

Remove most of the core of each apple, but leave a $^1/_2$ inch (1 cm) "plug" at the bottom. Set in a baking dish. Blend together the maple syrup, nuts, raisins or cranberries, butter and cinnamon. Divide mixture equally and spoon into apple cavities. Pour water around the apples to a depth of $^1/_4$ inch (6 mm). Bake at 375°F (190°C) for 45 minutes, or until apples are soft. Spoon apples and sauce into individual serving dishes. Serve with ice cream, drizzled with maple syrup.

Maple Poached Pears in White Wine

Team this classic dessert with biscotti or other crisp biscuits.

4 firm ripe pears	½ pt/300 ml white wine
4 whole cloves	water
1 cinnamon stick	2 tbsp/30 ml sliced almonds
4 fl oz/125 ml pure maple syrup	
(serves 4)	

Peel the pears and remove the cores but leave the stem in place. Stud a clove into each pear. Place the pears on their sides in an ovenproof dish. Place the cinnamon stick beside the pears. Blend the maple syrup and wine together and pour over the pears. Add water, if required, to ensure that the liquid is half covering the pears. Cover with foil and poach for about 1 hour at 375°F (190°C), basting occasionally. Remove cloves and cinnamon stick and spoon pears and sauce into individual serving dishes. Sprinkle with toasted, sliced almonds.

Maple Apple Blueberry Crisp

Maple syrup is the sweetener in both the filling and the crust of this delicious "comfort food" dessert.

1 lb/500 g sliced apples
1 tbsp/15 ml cornflour
1 tsp/5 ml cinnamon

approx 5 apples
= 4½ cup

oats: 1½ oz = ½ cup

½ pt/300 ml pure maple syrup
½ pt/300 ml blueberries, fresh or frozen
6 oz/180 g rolled oats   *2 cups*
2 oz/75 g plain flour
4 oz/120 g butter, softened
(serves 6)

Place the sliced apples in an 8 inch (20 cm) square pan. Whisk the cornflour and cinnamon into half the maple syrup. Pour the maple syrup mixture over the apples. Add the blueberries, stirring gently to mix together. In a small bowl, stir together the rolled oats and flour. Blend in the butter. Stir in the remaining maple syrup, then spread the rolled oat mixture evenly over the apples. Bake at 375°F (190°C) for 45 minutes or until crumb topping is browned.

French Canadian Maple Syrup Pie

This traditional recipe is so rich that only small serving pieces are needed. The recipe can be easily doubled.

1 oz/30 g plain flour	2 egg yolks, beaten lightly
4 fl oz/125 ml cold water	2 tbsp/30 ml butter
½ pt/300 ml pure maple syrup	1 baked 8 inch (20 cm) pie shell

Stir together the flour and water until smooth. In a heavy saucepan pour in the maple syrup. Stir the flour mixture into syrup, then add the beaten egg yolks. Cook over a low heat, stirring constantly, for about 5 minutes until thickened. Add the butter and stir until melted. Pour the mixture into the pie shell. Cool to room temperature before serving with whipped or ice cream.

Maple Pecan Pie with Chocolate Chunks

Melted chocolate chunks are a wonderful surprise in this delicious maple pecan pie.

3 squares (3 oz/90 g) bittersweet chocolate	3 eggs
3 oz/90 g chopped pecans	6 fl oz/175 ml pure maple syrup
1 9 inch (23 cm) unbaked, deep pie shell	1 tsp/5 ml vanilla
	2 tbsp/30 ml butter, melted

Cut the chocolate into chunks. Scatter the chocolate pieces and pecans over the unbaked pie shell. In a medium mixing bowl, beat the eggs with a whisk. Mix in the maple syrup, vanilla and melted butter and stir thoroughly. Pour the filling into the pie shell. Bake at 350°F (180°C) for 40 minutes or until centre is brown but not quite set (centre sets upon cooling). Cool on a rack.

Maple Mousse with Candied Pecans

The candied pecans in this melt-in-the-mouth mousse add a surprise crunchy texture – sure to please.

2¹/₂ oz/75 g pecan halves
¹/₂ pt/300 ml pure maple syrup
1 sachet unflavoured gelatin
3 tbsp/45 ml cold water

3 eggs, separated
¹/₂ pt/300 ml double or
whipping cream
6 pecan halves (optional garnish)

(serves 6)

Toast the pecans on a baking sheet at 350°F (180°C) for 5 minutes. Heat one-third of the maple syrup in a heavy medium saucepan until boiling. Boil rapidly for 4–5 minutes, stirring occasionally. Remove from the heat and add the pecans, stirring until they are evenly coated. Remove the pecans from the saucepan and allow to cool. Cut the candied pecans into small pieces and set aside. In a small bowl, sprinkle the gelatin into the cold water, then set aside. In a double boiler, mix together the remaining maple syrup and the egg yolks. Stir constantly for about 9 minutes until slightly thickened. Add the gelatin mixture and stir until dissolved, then remove from heat. Allow to cool in a large bowl until the mixture is the same consistency as unbeaten egg whites. Beat the egg whites until stiff. Beat cream until stiff. First, fold egg whites into the maple syrup mixture, then fold in the whipping cream. Add the candied pecans and stir until combined. Divide mousse between six serving dishes, then cover and chill for 3 hours.

Maple Walnut Torte

This is a favourite in most Canadian homes – a very rich and decadent dessert.

Base:	3 tbsp/45 ml pure maple syrup
3 oz/90 g butter	1 tbsp/15 ml corn syrup
2 oz/60 g sugar	2 tbsp/30 ml double cream
1 egg yolk	7 oz/210 g walnuts, coarsely
5 oz/150 g plain flour	chopped and toasted
Filling:	**Topping:**
4½ oz/135 g brown sugar	6 oz/180 g semi-sweet chocolate
2 oz/60 g butter	4 fl oz/125 ml double cream
(serves 8–10)	

Base: Preheat oven to 350°F (180°C). Cream together the butter and sugar until light and fluffy. Add the egg yolk and beat well. Stir in the flour until the mixture is blended and crumbly. Press firmly into a 10 inch (25 cm) springform cake tin. Ensure the mixture comes at least ½ inch (1 cm) up the sides of the cake tin. Bake for 12 minutes until lightly golden.

Filling: Combine the brown sugar, butter, maple syrup, corn syrup and cream in a heavy saucepan. Stir constantly and bring to a boil. Boil for 1 minute, then gently spread nuts over the base. Pour the filling evenly over the walnuts. Bake for 10 minutes or until bubbly. Allow to cool.

Topping: Melt the chocolate and cream together over a low heat, stirring until smooth. Spread chocolate over torte.

Cheesecake Blossom Tarts with Raspberries

For a stunning dessert, place raspberry *coulis* (*purée*) on the bottom of a dessert plate. Place the filo tart on top of *coulis* and garnish with additional raspberries.

Crust:	1 sachet of gelatin
6 sheets filo pastry, thawed	2 fl oz/60 ml cold water
2 oz/60 g butter, melted	4 fl oz/125 ml whipping cream
Filling:	12 oz/360 g raspberries,
8 oz/240 g cream cheese	fresh or frozen
6 fl oz/175 ml pure maple syrup	
(makes 12 tarts)	

Grease 12 muffin tin cups. Lay 3 filo sheets on a large cutting board and brush with some melted butter. Cut each sheet into 6 even rectangles. Fit a double layer of filo rectangles into 6 muffin cups. Then place a single rectangle into each muffin cup. Arrange the corners so they stick out in different directions and the cup is 3 filo layers thick. Repeat with remaining 6 muffin cups. Bake at 350°F (180°C) for 10 minutes or until golden. Cool for 10 minutes in the muffin tins, then remove and cool completely.

Filling: Beat the softened cream cheese with an electric mixer until smooth. Blend in the maple syrup. In a small pan, pour gelatin into cold water. Allow to stand for 5 minutes. Heat gelatin over a low heat, stirring until dissolved. Add the hot gelatin to cream cheese mixture and then fold in the whipped cream. Chill the mixture for about 15 minutes. When chilled, stir, then pour about 2 oz (60 g) of filling into each filo "blossom." Stand for 2 hours to set. Just before serving, divide raspberries between tarts.

Index